Searchlight BOOKS

Hunting and Fishing

Deer Hunting

Kyle Brach

Lerner Publications ◆ Minneapolis

Lerner Publications Company
An imprint of Lerner Publishing Group, Inc.
241 First Avenue North
Minneapolis, MN 55401 USA

For reading levels and more information, look up this title at www.lernerbooks.com.

Main body text set in Adrianna Regular.
Typeface provided by Chank.

Library of Congress Cataloging-in-Publication Data

Names: Brach, Kyle, author.
Title: Deer hunting / Kyle Brach.
Description: Minneapolis : Lerner Publications, [2024] | Series: Searchlight books. Hunting and fishing | Includes bibliographical references and index. | Audience: Ages 8–11 | Audience: Grades 4–6 | Summary: "In North America, deer are the most popular animal to hunt. And deer hunting has been practiced for centuries. From staying safe to protecting nature, readers will learn everything they should know about deer hunting"—Provided by publisher.
Identifiers: LCCN 2022044044 (print) | LCCN 2022044045 (ebook) | ISBN 9781728491561 (library binding) | ISBN 9798765603758 (paperback) | ISBN 9798765600436 (ebook)
Subjects: LCSH: Deer hunting—North America—Juvenile literature. | Deer hunting—Juvenile literature.
Classification: LCC SK301 .B693 2024 (print) | LCC SK301 (ebook) | DDC 639/.1165—dc23/eng/20230111

LC record available at https://lccn.loc.gov/2022044044
LC ebook record available at https://lccn.loc.gov/2022044045

Manufactured in the United States of America
1–CG–7/15/23

Table of Contents

Chapter 1

GOING DEER HUNTING

You've been in the tree stand for three hours, and so far . . . nothing. But wait! Is that movement about 100 yards (91.4 m) away? You bring your 20-gauge shotgun up into position. You look through your scope and see a deer. You place the crosshairs exactly where you want to shoot. You take aim . . . place your finger on the trigger . . . and fire!

Deer hunting is a popular outdoor sport.

Hunting relies on skills, instincts, and knowledge, and provides a thrilling adventure for millions of Americans every year. Of all the animals in the wild to hunt, deer are the most popular. With their keen senses of hearing and smell, they provide quite a challenge for hunters.

A female deer is called a doe. Baby deer are called fawns.

Different Types of Deer

There are five deer species in North America that are hunted. The white-tailed deer is the most widespread and most often hunted. They live in forests, swamps, fields, and prairies across the US, except for the Southwest, Hawaii, and Alaska. They are known for the white underside of their tails. They flash the white underside when they sense danger. They can weigh up to 300 pounds (136.1 kg).

Hunting History

In earlier times, Native Americans like the Choctaw Nation were known as skilled deer hunters. They knew how to use every part of the animals they hunted so nothing went to waste. Deer provided meat called venison that fed the Nation. Deer hide was used to make blankets, robes, shoes, and more. Tendons were used as bowstrings or sewing thread, and antlers made good garden rakes. Bones were turned into tools such as awls, needles, knives, combs, and fishhooks.

The Choctaw Nation used animal hides, such as deer hide, to make objects like this drum.

More Deer

The mule deer, also known as the black-tailed deer, has big ears like a mule. They are common in desert areas of the western US. They are the second-most popular deer for hunting. Moose are the largest deer in North America. They can weigh up to 1,800 pounds (816.5 kg) and stand close to seven feet (2.1 m) tall at the shoulders.

MOOSE HAVE POWERFUL SHOULDERS THAT MAKE THEM LOOK HUMPBACKED.

Hunters can look for elk
in mountainous areas.

Elk live in mountainous areas in the western US.
They can weigh up to 730 pounds (331.1 kg). Caribou,
or reindeer, are native to the northern parts of North
America in Alaska and the Canadian Rockies. They weigh
up to 400 pounds (181.4 kg).

The scope on a rifle makes targets look closer.

Hunting Gear

A successful hunt depends on having the right gear.
Your first decision is whether you'll use a gun or a bow.
If hunting with a gun, you'll most likely use a rifle or a
shotgun.

A rifle has a long barrel with grooves on the inside that shoots bullets. A metal case called a cartridge holds each bullet. A shotgun's long barrel is smooth on the inside. It can either shoot pellets made of steel or lead called shot or buckshot or a single projectile called a slug.

Young hunters should never handle a weapon without adult supervision.

Hunting with a Bow and Arrows

Bowhunting is one of the oldest types of hunting. Without the fire power of a gun, bowhunters must get closer to their prey. They may shoot from just 30 yards (27.4 m) away. Bowhunters must move quietly so they can get the best shot possible.

The riser is where you hold a compound bow. It provides stability for all the other parts.

ARROWS USED FOR HUNTING HAVE
RAZOR-SHARP BROADHEAD TIPS.

Bowhunters often use a compound bow, which uses wheels and cables to make it easier to pull back the string. Compound bows are great for young hunters since you can adjust them as you grow bigger and stronger.

Chapter 2

PLAY IT SAFE

Playing it safe means knowing how to use your weapon. It also means being prepared for bad weather and for finding your way.

Dress for Safety Success

Wearing camouflage helps hunters blend into the scenery so they can hide in plain sight from prey. While hunters don't want to be seen by deer, they do need to be seen by other hunters. That's why proper hunting gear includes bright orange hats, vests, or other garments. The bright color keeps hunters from mistaking you for a deer. And don't worry about the deer. They are colorblind and won't spot you.

Bright orange clothing helps keep hunters safe.

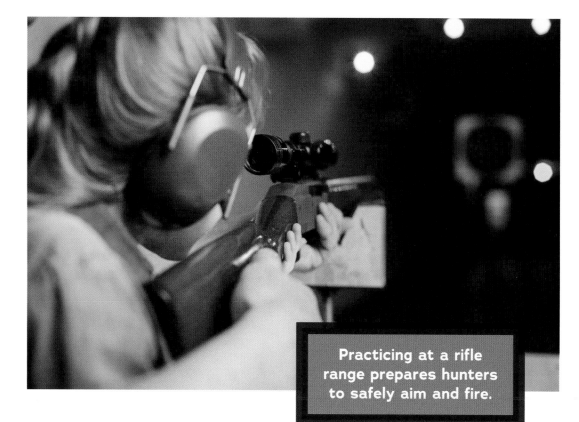

Practicing at a rifle range prepares hunters to safely aim and fire.

Gun Safety

Nothing prepares you for safe hunting better than knowing how to properly handle your shotgun or rifle. You need to practice at a range, and you should take lessons from a trusted adult or organization.

Gun safety is also about being aware of your surroundings. Pay attention to who and what is around you. Keep your gun's safety on and your finger off the trigger until you're ready to fire.

Bow and Arrow Safety

You will also need a lot of practice with a bow and arrow before you'll be ready to use them for hunting. Safety starts with keeping your arrows in a special container called a quiver until you are ready to use one. It also includes waiting to nock your arrow until you're ready to aim.

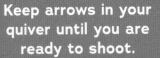

Keep arrows in your quiver until you are ready to shoot.

Experienced hunters know to pack essential gear.

More Ways to Stay Safe

Hunters must make sure someone at home knows exactly where they are and how long they will be hunting. It is also a good idea to pack a basic survival kit that includes extra drinking water, a fire-starting kit, a compass, a flashlight, and a smartphone. The biggest safety rule of hunting is to never shoot at anything unless you are 100 percent sure you know what it is.

STEM Spotlight

A deer will smell you before it sees or hears you. In fact, a deer can smell your stinky toes from 0.5 miles (0.8 km) away. It's their superpower. They use their sense of smell to make decisions that help them find food and keep them safe. But how and why can they smell so well?

Olfactory receptors are nerve cells found inside noses. These receptors receive and sense smells and instantly send messages to the brain. Humans have 5 million olfactory receptors, while deer have nearly 300 million olfactory receptors!

A deer has an excellent sense of smell.

Chapter 3

DEER HUNTING BASICS

Deer have excellent senses and will take off at the first sign of trouble. To hunt deer, you need to know their habits: where they eat, where they rest, where they travel. One way to do this is by scouting your hunting location ahead of time. Ask other hunters where they've had luck in the past. Find a field map and look for possible food and water sources.

Bucks rub their antlers on trees to mark their territory.

Scouting an area for deer means exploring and looking for clues. Look for deer tracks, deer droppings, and possible deer resting areas where the grass or undergrowth is flattened. Adult male deer, called bucks, will often rub their antlers on trees, about 2 to 4 feet (0.6 to 1.2 m) off the ground. These are called antler rubs, and if you see one, you know you are in a buck's territory.

Looking for Prey

One way to hunt deer is to walk around until you find one. This hunting technique is called still hunting. Still hunting involves moving around very slowly and quietly and making sure to always walk into the wind. This is so the wind won't carry human scents to unsuspecting deer.

Hunters must have patience while searching for deer.

Some hunters use trail cameras to monitor deer behavior.

When still hunting, hunters must make sure that even their clothes are quiet. Even the slightest rustling noise can scare away a deer. They walk extra carefully, trying not to crunch on leaves. Whenever they can they hide behind trees, bushes, and rocks to stay out of sight.

Waiting for Prey

Another way to hunt deer is to stay still. Hunters who prefer to remain in one spot often rely on stands or blinds to keep them hidden. Stands are platforms 10 to 15 feet (3.0 m to 4.6 m) above the ground in trees. From up there, deer cannot easily see you or smell you.

Deer stands hide hunters above the ground.

This portable deer blind sits on the ground.

Blinds are places where hunters can stay hidden on the ground. They can be natural features like trees, bushes, and hills, or they can be a tent-like structure that blends into the surrounding area.

Hunters who prefer to hunt this way need to scout their location carefully before setting up. There's no use setting up where there will be no deer.

Chapter 4

CONSERVE AND PROTECT

An ecosystem is all the living things in an area. A healthy ecosystem is in balance when there aren't too many or too few of any given plant or animal. Wildlife officials keep track of the number of deer in a given area. When there are more deer than there are natural resources to feed them, they count on hunters to keep the deer population in balance. Without hunters, there would be too many deer, which can lead to disease, hunger, and accidents with vehicles on roads.

Hunters will be able to enjoy the thrill of hunting year after year when they help preserve and protect the natural world. Deer hunters do this in many ways. One way is to pay for a state hunting license and tag fees. This money supports safety courses and the care of natural habitats. Hunters also donate to conservation and environmental organizations and pay special taxes on equipment.

Wildlife managers monitor deer populations.

Caring for nature helps keep the environment healthy for animals and people.

Caring for Nature

Hunters care about nature. They know it is important to leave it as you found it. When you are done for the day, you need to leave your location in its natural condition.

Model hunters respect private property. They don't litter or destroy posted signs. They are careful not to do anything that would harm the environment. This helps ensure that hunting remains an activity you and future generations can enjoy for years to come!

Hunting Hints

- Look for fresh deer droppings. They will be small, oval, and shiny.

- A white-tailed deer with its tail down feels unthreatened. If the tail is up with the white showing, it is on alert.

- Cover your odor with purchased scents. A drop or two of skunk scent is usually enough to fool a deer.

- If you hear a deer snort, they are warning others of danger.

Deer snort to warn their herd of danger.

Glossary

buckshot: many small balls, or pellets, of lead or metal shot from a shotgun

camouflage: clothes made from cloth in a mixture of colors, usually green and brown, that allow the wearer to blend in with natural surroundings

conservation: the protection of valuable things, especially forests, wildlife, and natural resources

ecosystem: a community of organisms and their environment

habitat: the place where an animal or plant lives in nature

nock: to fit an arrow to the bowstring to prepare to shoot

range: the longest distance at which a weapon can be used and still hit a target

safety: a device that keeps a gun from firing

scouting: gathering information about game animals in a specific area

slug: a single bullet or projectile that is fired from a shotgun

still hunting: moving silently and cautiously in pursuit of game

Learn More

Brach, Kyle. *Bowhunting*. Minneapolis: Lerner Publications, 2024.

Britannica Kids: Deer
https://kids.britannica.com/students/article/deer/273948

Britannica Kids: Hunting
https://kids.britannica.com/students/article/hunting/274993

Doyle, Abby Badach. *Deer Hunting*. New York: Gareth Stevens Publishing, 2023.

Kiddle: Hunting Facts for Kids
https://kids.kiddle.co/Hunting

Kingston, Seth. *Hunting*. New York: PowerKids Press, 2022.

Index

Photo Acknowledgments

Image credits: p. 5; Wild Media/Shutterstock, p. 6; Tony Campbell/Shutterstock, p. 7; Darla Hallmark/Dreamstime, p. 8; Harry Collins Photograph/Shutterstock, p. 9; Weekend Warrior Photos/Shutterstock, p. 10; Corepics Vof/Dreamstime, p. 11; Roman Kosolapov/Dreamstime, p. 12; Ben Schonewille/Shutterstock, p. 13; Bob Ross/Shutterstock, p. 15; CSNafzger/Shutterstock, p. 16; YAKOBCHUK VIACHESLAV/Shutterstock, p. 17; zeljkodan/Shutterstock; p. 18; New Africa/Shutterstock, p. 19; Rinus Baak/Dreamstime, p. 21; zeljkodan/Shutterstock, p. 22; PRESSLAB/Shutterstock, p. 23; Keith Bell/Shutterstock; p. 24; Aleksandar Milutinovic; p. 25; Jeffrey B Banke/Shutterstock, p. 27; Robert Bodnar T, p. 28; Ehrlif/Dreamstime, p. 29; Rademakerfotografie/Dreamstime.

Cover: Stephan Pietzko/Dreamstime.